The spiritual, scientific and economic importance of Maha Kumbh revealed through Scientific and ultra-Modern research Techniques

By Dr(Er) Om Prakash
Professor

Abstract

The spiritual, scientific and economic importance of Maha Kumbh is substantial, and so is its social harmony Every Hindu festival and ritual has a scriptural basis behind it. They are celebrated with zeal and enthusiasm as well as there exists a solid scientific, historical, and. philosophical basis. In a world characterized by the frenetic pace of modernity, there are few events that have the ability to unite millions of people in pursuit of a purpose larger than themselves. The Maha Kumbh Mela, a revered fair held four times over a period of 12 years, exemplifies this purpose. This research reveals the proven spiritual, scientific and economic importance of Maha Kumbh with the help of scientific and ultra-modern research techniques.

Keywords

Humongous gathering, Maha Kumbha, Pryagaraja, Sangam, Sustainable strategy, Civilization

Introduction

Every Hindu festival and ritual has a scriptural basis behind it. They are celebrated with zeal and enthusiasm and have a solid scientific, historical and philosophical basis. All these characteristics together provide a reason to celebrate a festival or perform a ritual. The purpose of these rituals is to lead a person on a spiritual path where they can achieve complete psychological balance, renewal and relaxation. The origin of Kumbha is very ancient and dates back to the time when the pitcher, which was offered to immortality, was found during the churning of the ocean. There was a fierce battle between the demons and the gods for this pitcher. To save the pitcher of nectar from the demons, the gods who were more powerful than the demons were entrusted with the protection of the pitcher, namely Brihaspati, Surya, Chandra and Shani. The four gods ran away to save the pitcher of nectar from the demons and during this time the demons chased the demons for 12 days and nights. During the chase, the demons kept the pitcher in Haridwar, Prayag, Ujjain and Natik. In memory of this sacred ceremony, Kumbh is celebrated at these 4 places every 12 years (Bhardwaj, 1973). As the great Hindu saint, Adi Shankaracharya, said:

"कुम्भे स्नानं तर्पणं दानं, यज्ञो व्रतं तपः श्रेष्ठम्।" "Kumbhe snanam tarpanam danam, yajno vratam tapah shreshtham." That means: "Bathing in the Kumbh, offering oblations, charity, performing sacrifices, observing vows, and practicing austerities are considered the most superior acts."

A total of 600 million tourists are estimated to participate throughout the entire festival. To accommodate the massive influx of pilgrims , authorities have established a temporary city spanning 4,000 hectares. Uttar Pradesh Chief Minister Yogi Adityanath said "62 crore devotees have come to the Maha Kumbh so far and the gathering of such a large number of people during a certain period is in itself" "one of the rarest events of the century". [2]

History of Maha-Kumbh

According to religious texts, it is believed that the first Kumbh was organized during the reign of King Harshavardhan (7th century AD). The famous Chinese traveler Hiuen Tsang has mentioned about the organization of Kumbh Mela while describing his visit to India. Along with this, he has also mentioned the generosity of King Harshavardhan. Hiuen Tsang has said that King Harshavardhan used to organize a big event at the confluence of rivers every five years, in which he used to donate his entire wealth to the poor and religious people. According to the texts, Kumbh also finds its reference in Ramcharitamans when sage Yajnavalaksy demystifies the Lord Vishnu's Avatar as Shri Rama. When there is a great gathering, apparently at Maha Kumbha many sages appear at Pryagaraja. When Sage Bharadwaj asks the significance of Rama Avatar, sage Yajnavakya tells the whole story at this great confluence. Then Rishi Valmiki himself makes reference to Maha Kumbha (Bhardwaj, 1973).

The Maha-Kumbh festival has its roots in Hindu mythology, dating back to the Samudra Manthan, or the churning of the ocean. According to legend, the gods and demons collaborated to churn the ocean, producing the nectar of immortality, Amrita. However, the demons attempted to steal the Amrita, leading to a fierce battle.

To prevent the demons from obtaining the Amrita, the gods hid it in four different locations, which are now the sites of the Kumbh Mela: Haridwar, Prayagraj, Nashik, and Ujjain.[3] Furthermore, according to the scriptures, Kumbh is organized in these coincidences. Kumbh is organized on the banks of Ganga in Haridwar when Jupiter enters Aquarius and Sun enters Aries. Secondly, when Jupiter enters Aries and Sun and Moon are in Capricorn, Kumbh is organized at Triveni Sangam in Prayagraj on the new moon day. Third Kumbh, when Jupiter and Sun enter the Sun sign, Kumbh is organized on the banks of Godavari in Nashik and when Jupiter and Sun enter the Sun sign, Kumbh is organized at river Shipra Banks in Ujjain (Bhardwaj, 1973).

Maha Kumbh festival is a testament of grandeur and spiritual vibrancy of India. As of today the Maha Kumbh has attracted **crores and crores of devotees from 14 January 2025. Single day is** alone is witnessed **5 crore** devotees. But, a total and a total **number of 50 crore devotees** are **expected upto the day of Maha Shivratri i.e. 26th February.** Many dignitaries have arrived already and in one occasion, a **21-member delegation from 10 countries** appeared at the Sangam on January 16,

2025. These were from **Fiji, Finland, Guyana, Malaysia, Mauritius, Singapore, South Africa, Sri Lanka, Trinidad and Tobago, and the UAE. They appreciated their** presence at the heritage site Their arrangements were made at the **Tent City** in **Arail**.

As the great Indian sage, Swami Vivekananda, said: "The Kumbh Mela is a symbol of the eternal quest of the human soul for immortality and liberation." The Maha Kumbh Mela 2025 is considered the most auspicious of all Kumbh Melas due to its unique celestial alignments and historical significance. Unlike regular Kumbh Melas, which occur every 12 years at four sacred locations—Prayagraj, Haridwar, Ujjain, and Nashik—the Maha Kumbh Mela is a rare event that happens once every "144 years". The next Maha Kumbh after 2025 will not occur until 2169, making this gathering exceptionally significant for devotees.[4]

In the world's largest human gathering in history, which is at current Mahakumbh Mela, Prayagaraj, 2025, one witnesses not just a religious congregation, but also a sustainable Civilisation.

MahaKumbha - A blueprint of the society.

Maha Kumbh Mela has been described as a blueprint for sustainable civilization by many top Celebrities who have visited the sacred place during Mahakumbh. They even highlighted its impact on human consciousness. Mahakumbh signifies India's soft power, true legacy, and leadership through service. This research paper highlights the importance of MahaKumbh Mela's principles in formulating sustainable resource management, inclusive growth , and synchronized mass collaboration. In the world's largest human gathering in history, which is at current Mahakumbh Mela, Prayagaraj, 2025, one witnesses not just a religious congregation, but also a blueprint for sustainable civilisation. Whilst India marches towards being a global superpower, one must also keep into one's remembrance that India's strength lies not just in what it builds, but in what it preserves. Mahakumbbh Mela celebrated from time immemorial, and evidenced by several ancient shastras has in itself proven that it is a perpetual event. In this descriptive research paper, the methodology adopted is to understand the sustainability model of this event. Every 144 years the cycle repeats itself and at any given point in time, it is the largest gathering ever in the History of mankind. Undoubtedly, it does serve as a blueprint for sustainable humongous gathering that can be replicated to develop a strategy to control vast CO-EXISTENCE.

Planning and sustainability

"Hum Itihas batate nahi, Itihas Likhte hai, Itihas Banate hain" There are celebrities and what they say or do is History, just like Happening at Mahakumbha that transforms itself into History. Gautam Adani says is making History. Gautam Adani visited Maha Kumbh Mela, describing it as a blueprint for sustainable civilization. He highlighted its impact on human consciousness. He emphasized the significance of India's soft power, true legacy, and leadership through service. Adani stressed the importance of the Kumbh Mela's principles in creating inclusive growth, sustainable resource management, and harmonious mass collaboration. Fresh from paying a visit to Maha Kumbh Mela in Prayagraj, billionaire Gautam Adani said that the world's largest human gathering is not just religious but a blueprint for sustainable civilisation. "As India marches towards becoming a global superpower, we must remember: our strength lies not just in what we build, but in what we preserve," he said. "The Kumbh isn't just a religious gathering - it's a blueprint for sustainable civilisation." Evidently, his comments summarizes the preparedness at humongous gathering at Mahakumbha (The Economics Times News, Jan 27, 2025).

The government dynamically upgrades their **meticulous arrangement** to organize this humongous arrival of pilgrims. A craze of waves and waves of oceans of pilgrims are arriving and though one hears of some or other occasional mishaps, but, those who visited appear to be tremendously satisfied. They tell their stories as if they have achieved a medal and show-off a victory of a sort. Kudos then to the Uttar Pradesh Government, Agencies and independent organizers that have supported the arrival, stay and departure of this oceanic waves of pilgrimage. At the same time, this unpredictable and exponentially increasing numbers does ion involve cutting-edge **technology**, **infrastructural** enhancement, and **sustainable planning. Besides some stray incidents, this level arrangements** set a benchmark in event management. Holy **Snans** and presence of vibrant **Akharas,** digital innovation and transformations display large-scale sustainability initiatives (Chadha & Onkar, 2016).

Mahakumbha displays a vibrant tapestry of faith, culture, and innovation. There is a remarkable presence of "**Tejas Pandal**," which is a superb **85 feet tall superstructure** replicating **HALs Tejas fighter jet**. Then there are pan India **Akharas** considered the custodians of both spiritual and holy tradition. Mahakumbha also offers artisans a terrific base where they can showcase their talent over "**One District, One Product**" platform. Then **Kalagram** offers a live cradle of par excellence crafts, luscious cuisine & culture (Chandan, S., & Kumar, A. (2019).

On the technical front jaw-dropping drones captivate the heart of the audience as they depict the mythical "**Prayag Mahatmyam**" and "**Samudra Manthan**." Furthermore, one witnesses "**cultural extravaganza**" ft. Shankar Mahadevan, Mohit Chauhan, Kailash Kher, and host of others with spiritual fervor. This is a prototype of a civilization of the future, given that population keeps increasing at a present rate.

One can notice how the everyday roads are getting crowded by the day. The roads which looked deserted 10 years ago are witnessing damning jams today. By analysing the management, mishaps, successes and failures at Mahakumbh, one can offer a blueprint of tomorrow. From 8 billion population as of today, one can optimistically assume 10 billion in 2050 to almost 15 billion in 2100. But, the density of population increase can be predictably very high in India as the density may observe an exponential growth. The population in the world scenario may double but the concentration at some urban areas in India can be 4-6 times (Chandan & Kumar, (2019).

Learning and Scrutiny

Using some AI algorithm like regression or even ANN, one can predict the availability of resources in the ever increasing population scenario. Analysis of supply chain management and Logistics complex at Mahakumbh, therefore, is extremely necessary for sustainable development. For example, how one can achieve increasing boarding and lodging facility. Similar, waste management assumes equal importance. Environment degradation analysis, pre and post Kumbh, river water analysis pre and post Kumbh, and environment noise and pollution analysis attains tremendous importance if one needs to develop sustainable strategies to preserve the quality living of the citizens (David & Roy, 2016)

Major dates for sacred bath and Their Significance in terms of data analytics

Within the heavy crowding and traffic some days achieve peak presence due to particular days. Mahakumbha accompanies with its sacred bathing ritual (The holy Snan). Following are the dates of Holy Snans:

Date January 29, 2025: Mauni Amavasya is a day steeped in significance, as it is believed that the celestial alignments are most propitious for the sacred act of bathing in the holy river. It commemorates a profound event when Rishabh Dev, revered as one of the first sages, broke his protracted vow of silence and immersed himself in the purifying waters of the Sangam. As a result, Mauni Amavasya draws the largest congregation of pilgrims to the Kumbh Mela, making it a momentous day of spiritual devotion and purification.

February 3, 2025: Basant Panchami symbolizes the transition of seasons and celebrates the arrival of the Goddess of Knowledge, Saraswati, in Hindu mythology.

February 12, 2025: Maghi Purnima is renowned for its connection with the veneration of Guru Brahaspati and the belief that the Hindu deity Gandharva descends from the heavens to the sacred Sangam.

February 26, 2025 Maha Shivratri holds deep symbolism as it marks the final holy bath of the Kalpvasis, and it is intrinsically connected to Lord Shankar.

Nurturing Kumbha in a Secular World

Although some consider the Kumbh Mela to be sacred, for many it is nothing but a strange and bizarre superstition-filled gathering filled with meaningless rituals, pollution, exploitation and social stratification. Therefore, to understand the rationale behind the Kumbh Mela, it is more important to see it from the perspective of the people themselves.

Though Kumbh Mela is considered the world's largest congregation due to its antiquity, diversity and scale, it has been questioned a lot in the present times. This is because in today's times, there is a widespread tendency to seek rationality and logic in everything, whereas if seen in the true sense, most of our lives are irrational like emotions. Needless to mention, people all over the world will view Kumbh Mela from the rationale of their own secular world views. There are many other ways of looking at it, such as feminist, Marxist, socialist, Freudian and many more. Though some consider Kumbh Mela to be sacred, for many it is just a strange and bizarre convention full of superstition, meaningless rituals, pollution, exploitation and social stratification. Therefore, it is more important to see it from our perspective to understand the rationale behind Kumbh Mela. Moreover, we may run the risk of a similar fate someday in Sabarimala, where the matter of tradition is completely ignored.

Nothing can be said with certainty about when the Kumbh Mela started. But it can be said with confidence that it is an ancient tradition in itself, which has been going on unbroken for more than ten thousand years. It is held every third year at four different places: Haridwar, Prayagraj, Nashik and Ujjain. Thus, every 12th year the Maha Kumbh Mela is held at these four places. The Ardh Kumbh Mela is held every two years at only two places, Hardwar and Prayagraj. These four places have four different rivers: the Ganges at Haridwar, the confluence of the Ganges, Yamuna and the extinct Saraswati at Prayagraj, the Godavari at Nasik and the Shipra at Ujjain. The fair at Haridwar is held when Jupiter is in Aquarius and is therefore known as Kumbh. The Nashik and Ujjain fairs are usually held before or after the monsoons and Jupiter is in Leo at this time, so it is called the Simhastha Kumbh Mela. The fair at Pragraj is held in winter and Jupiter is in the month of Magh at this time. That is why it is also called Magh Mela. In today's era, all the four fairs are called Kumbh. This year, more than 12 crore visitors are expected to come to the Ardh Kumbh to be celebrated in Prayagraj. According to this, it is the biggest religious festival in the world.

Rationale for the ritual

Kumbh Mela is a ritual in which satsang, puja, seva and bathing in the river are considered sacred. Most people who consider themselves modern support spiritual practices like yoga and meditation but disregard religious practices like rituals. Historically, criticism of idol worship by other religions has also served to promote a reaction against rituals. Swami Dayanand Saraswati, who founded the Arya Samaj, was also against idol worship. Even Mahatma Gandhi was against it. However, rituals have a specific purpose stated in Hindu scriptures and have a rational explanation. It is as integral a part of the process leading to self-realization as yoga and meditation. So let's talk about it in detail.

Hindu cosmic reality rejects the idea of an extra-cosmic God. Reality is a cosmic conscious principle that is uncreated, indestructible and omnipresent. It is called Brahman and is not to be confused with Brahma, the creator of the Hindu trinity. Everything created in the universe is a manifestation of Brahman, from whom everything arises, in whom everything resides and in whom everything dwells. The universe, nature and man are one. Everything dwells in Brahman. The very first verse of the Isho-Upanishad says:

"Everything that moves in this universe, including the movement of the universe itself, is in Him and resides in Him."

Brahman Hindu thought leads to moksha or self-realization. It is a purpose of life and a state where we experience oneness with the unity and wisdom of the universe and there is no separation between us and Brahman. This idea is succinctly summed up in four Upanishadic mahavakyas:

Prajna Brahman of Aitereya Upanishad explains that consciousness is Brahman

Ayam Atma Brahman of the Mandukya Upanishad states that individual consciousness and cosmic consciousness are the same

Tat Tvam Asi, this famous verse from Chandogya Upanishad says that you can realize that you are the same

"Aham Brahmasmi" from the Brihadaranyaka Upanishad is the blissful expression of that which one has realized, is Brahman.

There are many references in the scriptures on the role of karma (rituals, sacrifices and worldly actions) and jnana (knowledge and meditation) in attaining moksha or self-realization. Both practices are part of the eternal debate between outer and inner life. Scholars have said that those who focus solely on outer life get caught in an endless web of craving and ultimately suffering, while those who focus only internally become remote and reclusive. Hence the scriptures point to both karma and jnana together. The twelfth verse of the Isha Upanishad points to this:

"Those who worship the material world enter into deep darkness. Those who take pleasure in opposing the material world enter into even greater darkness."

Rituals prepare us for knowledge by enabling Chitta Shuddhi or purification of the mind. An agitated mind can never be contemplative. When we practice rituals we turn our thoughts away from the temptations and distractions of worldly activities, imbibe higher thoughts, serve others and thus calm our mind. A person with a calm mind is better equipped to pursue higher knowledge and meditation.

A cricket player has to first play for the school team, junior team and state team, only then can they play for the country. Similarly, rituals are the first step in the journey to moksha or self-realization.

Those who meditate should not impose their practice on those who are not yet ready for it. Instead of ridiculing those who perform rituals, they should heed Krishna's advice in the Bhagavad Gita (III.2.2)

"No wise man should try to disturb the mind of an ignorant person. Those who are associated with karma should try to complete all those tasks with devotion."

Superstition or deep astronomy knowledge?

It is said that if we bathe in holy rivers during Kumbh Mela, we attain salvation. Those who consider rituals irrational may consider this as superstition. However, it would be perfectly reasonable to ask if there is any rational explanation for this. According to Surya Shastra, the Panch-tatvas are most active at various places of Kumbh Mela due to the planetary configurations at that time. Moreover, among all the elements, water is the element that has the strongest memory power. Scientific research is going on to understand this quality of water. Homeopathy has always supported this. Moreover, there are many examples from ancient India, which were not understood by science earlier, but are now scientifically accepted. For example, non-dual consciousness or what Vedanta calls Brahman, is a field of scientific study today. Bathing during the Mela season with reverence or devotion removes the sanskaras and vasanas and frees the devotee from accumulated karmas. Rivers are considered holy because of the healing power of the river and the philosophy of unity. This is the significance of the Kumbh Mela. Like most Hindu traditions, the Kumbh Mela also has a scriptural explanation.

There is a logical explanation for the fact that Kumbh Mela lasts forty-five days on average. The reason is that Jupiter starts moving away from Aquarius after forty-five days.

Academic and media interest in the Kumbh Mela

When the Harvard Kumbh Mela Project came to light, it caught the attention of Rajiv Malhotra. In a 2015 article titled "Why the Kumbh Mela is at Risk", he wrote that Western intervention in Indian culture has a long history. It starts in a benign fashion but soon takes a dangerous turn. Academics, leftists, missionaries and institutions study and research Hindu traditions without the exaggerated spiritual significance of the Western perspective and the result is predictable. It always points out caste inequalities, gender discrimination, individual, environmental and public health concerns over religion. This criticism often leads to secularism without paying attention to the philosophical aspects which paves the way for the entry of Christian missionaries. We have recently seen how the issue of so-called gender discrimination led to the desecration of Sabarimala, an important Hindu pilgrimage site.

This research proposal on the Kumbh Mela from the Harvard South Asian Institute highlights Malhotra's research paper. According to the research:

"The fair inspires interdisciplinary research in many complementary fields. Pilgrimage and religious studies, public health, design, communication, business, and infrastructure engineering are just some of the many disciplines for which the fair creates a complex environment that can be understood through rigorous documentation and mapping."

Some of the things the researchers propose to study are:

1. How do groups of pilgrims from different economic and social backgrounds relate to each other? Is there a stratification within it that differentiates different types of pilgrims from one another?

2. How does the Mela reconcile the tension between its identity, national and religious identity?

3. Who are its major religious organs (individuals and institutions) and what influence do they have on the larger population? What are the differences in their relations with pilgrims, tourists, the press and the mela's governing organisations?

4. Public health concerns and environmental pollution

The media response so far has been mixed. While a large section has praised the excellent facilities and administration, some have also tried to create a negative perception.

BBC News on 14 January praised the infrastructure, good transport and accommodation, excellent sanitation, security, food supplies and improvements in hospital infrastructure.

On the other hand, Business Standard has tried to create a negative perception. On January 22, through an editorial titled "Can Kumbh Mela solve Uttar Pradesh's unemployment problem?", it has tried to show that the reason for such a large number of devotees attending this fair is large scale unemployment. In this way, instead of showing the sanctity of Kumbh Mela, an attempt has been made to show it in a negative light by linking it with unemployment.

Another Business Standard article published by Reuter on December 21 is titled, Sanctity and politics: Over 10 crore people to attend Kumbh in January. The article tries to politicise the Kumbh by saying that the Ardh Kumbh Mela is being promoted to boost the waning popularity of the Hindu nationalist BJP government by celebrating Hindu supremacy and marginalising Muslim unity. But the reality is that the Kumbh Mela has never witnessed communal tension.

On January 20, The Indian Express carried an article titled: The people keeping Kumbh clean. The article spread the rumour that 22,000 sanitation workers were cleaning toilets used by rich pilgrims.

Rajiv Malhotra warns of how Christian missionaries enter and operate in places where Hindus gather in large numbers. An article in the Nagaland Post urges the Naga delegation invited to the Kumbha Sanskruti Mela to showcase Naga culture so that it can spread the gospel of Jesus Christ. It considers it its birthright to spread the message of Jesus and hopes that one day the Kumbha Mela will turn into a great mission centre.

As the first part of the evangelistic Project Joshua II, the First Baptist Church of Nashville, Tennessee has adopted towns where the Kumbh Mela takes place and has been actively converting locals so that visitors face extreme difficulty trying to find services and supplies during their next visit. They are forming their own separate groups and raising their voices as well. It seems that a good section of the media is also on their side to such an extent that any section opposing their activity finds itself branded as an extremist image in the news media.

Arguments against migration of Kumbh Mela

From the above discussion I have taken the main themes of defaming Kumbh Mela by secular minded and evangelicals:

1.	Not trying to understand the subjective and spiritual nature of the Kumbh Mela takes it into the realm of superstition.
2.	Without understanding the synthesis achieved by Hinduism, the story of caste and class tensions serves to divide society rather than unite it.
3.	Hinduism's concern with the subjugation of individualism is actually the realization of the highest individualism.
4.	Giving more importance to public health concerns and environmental issues than celebrating the festival.
5.	Entering the Kumbh Mela with the intention of converting non-believers rather than respecting their faith

Let us analyse each topic briefly:

1 Not trying to understand the subjective nature of the Kumbh Mela results in it falling into the realm of superstition.

We have seen that Kumbh Mela is a ritual and rituals have an important role in the pursuit of spirituality. The scriptures explain the astronomical connections as to why rivers acquire healing properties under certain conditions. Satsang or a large gathering of people for a sacred purpose produces beneficial vibrations.

At the peak of the hippie era in the US in 1969, a famous music festival called Woodstock was held. Over 500,000 young people attended the five-day festival. Many famous musicians of the time performed at the festival. Woodstock has been portrayed as a landmark event, setting an example of peace and love in an otherwise contentious world. The Kumbh Mela is about three hundred times larger and nine times longer and has been an example of harmony, peace and diversity for thousands of years. If one looks at the Kumbh Mela from this perspective, it can be researched to understand the spiritual aspects of the Kumbh Mela using secular epistemology. Scientists can research whether the character of the river changes during such celestial events. Does the brain-mold of participants change during the Kumbh Mela? Does the personal aura expand? Spiritual progress can be measured on the scale of changes in various gunas (sattva, rajas, tamas). What happens to the quotient of mental awakening and emotional well-being? Such in-depth research will bridge the body of knowledge and secular research methods that will be useful in understanding the effects of subjectivity.

2 Without understanding the synthesis achieved by Hinduism, the narrative of

caste and class tensions serves to divide rather than unite society

The great thing about Kumbh Mela is its unifying power. Castes, classes, sadhus, siddhas, gender-mixers, all live together and bathe in the same river. It is the greatest display of diversity in unity on the entire planet. To turn this idea into social tension is a problem of the attitude of the observer of the event and not of the fair. For too long the whole meaning of Hinduism has been reduced to caste tensions and this may be the reason why the unifying principle of the religion is often overlooked.

In 2017 UNESCO inscribed the Kumbh Mela as an Intangible Cultural Heritage of Humanity. The intergovernmental committee observed: "The Kumbh Mela is the largest congregation of pilgrims on earth. The festival…reflects harmonious rituals and worship in sacred rivers..It is compatible with existing human rights instruments, as people from all walks of life participate in the festival on equal terms without any discrimination. As a religious festival, the tolerance and inclusiveness that the Kumbh Mela embodies are particularly valuable for the contemporary world"

3 Whether the person is colonized by religion

This modern idea of the separation of the individual from religion requires an intellectual discussion. According to Vivekananda, the Hindu idea that you are a universal individual can be frightening to some. People troubled by this idea ask if it leads to the loss of an individuality. Vivekananda asks what individuality is, . If the idea of individuality is rooted in the body you would lose it if you lost a part of the body. If it is in habit, an alcoholic would not change his habit for fear of losing his individuality. Vivekananda instead suggests that it is the universal that enjoys true individuality. At the level of self-realization multiplicity dissolves into unity. So apart from losing the individual idea the Hindu idea is an attempt to gain it:

"We are not yet individuals. We are striving toward individuality, and that is the infinite, that is the true nature of man." (CWSV- Book 2 p. 80)

4 Giving more importance to public health concerns and environmental issues than celebrating the festival

Realistically, large numbers of people celebrating Kumbh for thousands of years have not gotten sick. Scientists can study why the river is not harmful to health despite pollution. Moreover, if the study is aimed at finding scientific solutions to problems, it is welcome. But if it becomes a tool to thwart tradition then it is problematic.

5 Converts attempt to enter Kumbh Mela and convert non-religious people

There are two separate issues here. One is the Christian belief that their perceived truth is the only truth and thus they are compelled to use any means to bring others to their side. The second issue is more sociological. We need to examine what such a belief means to the fabric of human society.

To analyse the first issue I look at Swami Vivekananda. The need for religion arises because even the best secular knowledge does not satisfy our thirst. We crave for the ultimate knowledge, which answers all our questions. We find this idea in every religion and that is why religions claim superiority over secular knowledge. But in this battle between religious and secular knowledge, secular knowledge often wins because it is equipped with logic and epistemology. As the age of reason increases, people become disillusioned with 'believing in anything' and religions have not offered any effective alternative to this.

There is also a fight among religions to claim superiority over each other. However, the evidence they give for this is unsatisfactory. They say my ideology is superior because my book says so. Today, in the age of logic, this is not acceptable. But is there any other way to do this? If every religion is ready to prove itself right like science. Religions should come forward to such scrutiny.

Vivekananda explains two principles of logic. The first is that any particular idea is explained by general ideas. In other words any particular idea must be rationally generalized. For example if an apple falls, it may be a strange phenomenon, but if all apples fall, it means that there is some fundamental law acting upon it, in this case the law is gravity. The second principle is that the explanation of an event must be internal. In our example of the apple, if you throw an apple and it falls you may believe that a ghost pulled it down. This is an external explanation and to the rational mind it is not logical. But gravity is an internal explanation for this event, it is the nature of the thing itself. In all kinds of sciences we find that events are explained by what is going on within it.

Now we apply this principle to the God of Christianity, who resides outside the universe, and who wants to penetrate the inner conscious principles of Hinduism. Christianity believes that their God, sitting outside the universe, created the universe out of nothing and He Himself is outside it. This defies the principle of immanence. You can extend everything up to a point but then there is a dead end because God is outside everything. This is inconsistent with the 'First Principle of Logic' itself. On the other hand, Brahman is the origin of everything that exists here. It is thus consistent with the 'First Principle of Logic'. The second principle, that the explanation of a phenomenon must be internal, the theory of God sitting outside the universe does not stand up to it. This explanation of creation is like a ghost pulling down an apple. Brahman, on the other hand, is the proper explanation of that situation. As we saw in the verse of Isa Upanishad, it affects the whole creation. Everything originates from this, everything resides in this and merges back into this.

So Christians claim that, in their case, reason is not the basis of truth, so we have to reduce it to the realm of faith and dogma. Their logic behind intruding into other religions is intrinsically and irreparably flawed. I also want to say that Hindu philosophy is not against other philosophies. If a belief consoles its followers then let them believe in it. What I mean here is against the superiority of Christianity over other faiths and not Christianity itself.

Besides, history is proof that aggressive behaviour creates tension in the fabric of society which leads to violence and wars. Therefore, for the sake of harmony, the aggressive approach of these religions must end. It is also completely justified that the culture which is being subjected to aggression should build a protective shield around itself for self-defence and use all legitimate means against aggression.

Why and how should Kumbh Mela be protected and nurtured?

Kumbh Mela is a microcosm of Hindu cosmology. It demonstrates the unity of creation and the interdependence of celestial bodies and life. It celebrates unity with joy and enthusiasm without any gender and class based discrimination. Peace and brotherhood are celebrated on a much bigger scale than the Woodstock festival. It is the biggest living example of integrating diversity into unity. For this reason the *Intergovernmental Committee for the Safeguarding of the Intangible Cultural Heritage* under UNESCO has placed Kumbh Mela on the Representative List of the Intangible Cultural Heritage of Humanity.

The alleged distortion of the Kumbh Mela by other ideological perspectives naturally worries concerned Hindus. We must have a clear understanding of how to respond to these alleged threats in a way that is consistent with our identity. First, we must understand that criticism of Hinduism is nothing new. In ancient times, the materialist philosophy of Charvaka severely attacked Hinduism. Later, Hinduism survived attacks and subjugation by both Islam and Christianity. My argument is that we must respond to current challenges in a manner consistent with the strengths of Hinduism.

At the spiritual level, the knowledge of Dharma is inherent in the universe. It is not something that Hindus have imagined. It is self-evident and can be experienced by anyone who tries. Hence, Dharma is indestructible. We should use this realization as a strength to work towards the renaissance of Dharma.

The best way to defend religion at the intellectual level is through logic. Control the narrative with intellectual power. Let us be inspired by our ancient and modern sages. Find the logic behind the myriad Hindu practices and present it logically. The search for deeper meaning is fundamental. Present Hinduism as a way to find answers to the deepest questions of humanity.

At the level of existence, we must protect Hindu religions from other aggressive ideologies. Freedom of religion does not mean intrusion into the religious environment of other people. A culture that has been exploited has the right to vigilant and legal protection.

If we want the greatest festival on earth to be celebrated in all its glory in this holy land, we must work together and smartly to safeguard the Kumbh Mela and its system in the present and the future.

The UP Government and its agencies attempted to provide facilities for:

Security & Pilgrim Management: Hi-tech reconnaissance drones, digital monitoring,

- **Lodging**: Mahakumbha Nagar transformation to an actual city has been achieved with hundreds of thousands of tents and shelters/ Some are luxurious, deluxe and super deluxe tents.
- **Akashvani Kumbhvani** is also a remarkable innovation to provide vital information to pilgrims. There is this radio channel having timely **News Bulletins broadcasted live** at the strategic points at the Mahakumbh Nagar.
- **More e-buses**: about fifteen new e-buses deployment is made at the site. The shahi Snan dates have thirty plus more. These buses are twelve meter long with a single charge offering a 200 kilometer run (Kanaujiya & Tiwari.2022).
- 120 more Double Decker Buses are also added.
- **Maha Kumbh Mela App**: the app is from Indian Railways with a free helpline number, a supporting website, and facilitating transport info.

Nourishing the multitudes : Food Availability, Safety and Security Measures

and collaborative law enforcement facility. Security enhanced with **50k** police personnel and para military forces. There are also **14k** home guards and monitoring upgraded with 3k AI-based CCTV camera deployment. Furthermore, there are state-of-the-art Multi-Disaster Response vehicles for immediate disaster management (Greenough, P. G. (2013).

- **Infrastructure** projects include addition of **14** more flyovers, **9** moreghats, **7** more bus stations, scores of special trains, and also a stretch of over **12** KM new ghats. There are **200** more roads that are duly added (Forouhar & Hasankhani, 2018).
- **Navigational enhancements**: Over **800 multilingual signage** installed for the benefits of pilgrims. A **mobile app** created to provide **real time update** on crowd density, emergency alert, direction assistance, and boarding/lodging availability updates.
- **Healthcare & Sanitary**: Healthcare facility featured **6k more** beds, **43 more** clinics and **hospitals**. About **10k** sanitary helpers and **2k Ganges Sevaduts** deployment for maintaining sanitation dat the area (Holman & Shayegan, 2014).

A facility of free meals for 50 K people is being provided daily. Distribution of about **25 k ration cards** have also been provided. Moreover, **35 K new gas cylinders** have been provided and **4k new connections are offered**. A facility providing the daily **refilling of 5k gas cylinders is offered.** About 100k temporary food stalls have been facilitated for the public benefit. To enhance sanitation, health care and hygiene a very stringent food safety measure is implemented. This is possible through the Food safety officers who regularly survey food hygiene at various outlets. They have also fashioned mobile "**Food Safety on Wheels**" labs that conduct on-spot tests to ensure proper food safety. **This ensures that** every meal is safe for consumption and is hygienic (Houghton, 1994).

Spiritual Significance of Maha-Kumbh

The Maha-Kumbh festival holds immense spiritual significance in Hinduism. It is believed that the festival provides an opportunity for devotees to attain spiritual enlightenment and liberation. The ritual bathing in the sacred rivers is believed to purify the soul and wash away sins. By bathing in the Maha-Kumbh, people believe they can attain peace and prosperity.[5] Many people who visited there told that they left alcohol and non-veg eating after taking holy dip. It shows that it provides peace and purifies the soul. The festival also provides an opportunity for devotees to seek the blessings of the gods and goddesses and to attain spiritual growth.

As the great Hindu scripture, the Bhagavad Gita, says: "मोक्षस्य मार्ग प्रवक्ष्यामि, यज्ज्ञात्वा मोक्ष्यसे अशुभात्।" "Mokshasya margam pravakshyami, yajjnatva mokshyase ashubhat." That means: "I shall teach you the path of liberation, by knowing which you shall attain liberation from all sins." The Maha-Kumbh festival is also a celebration of the guru-shishya parampara, or the tradition of spiritual discipleship. The festival provides an opportunity for devotees to seek the guidance of spiritual leaders and to learn about the ancient traditions and customs of Hinduism. A total of 600 million tourists are estimated to participate throughout the entire festival. [1]

•Scientific significance of Maha-Kumbh :

Recent scientific studies have shed light on the significance of the Maha-Kumbh festival from a scientific perspective. Research has shown that the ritual bathing in the sacred rivers has a positive impact on the mental and physical health of devotees. People who visited there shared their experiences and told that many of them changed their disturbed routine to disciplined one and got more productive after taking the holy dip. The festival has also been shown to have a positive impact on the local environment, with the ritual bathing helping to purify the water and reduce pollution.[6] Uttar Pradesh Chief Minister Yogi Adityanath , Speaking in the Uttar Pradesh Assembly The State Pollution Control Board is regularly checking the water to maintain its quality. As per today's reports, the amount of BOD (biochemical oxygen demand) near Sangam is less than three, and the dissolved oxygen is around 8-9. It signifies that that the Sangam is water is suitable not just for bathing but also for aachman [a holy dip in which devotees also sip the water]," said Mr. Adityanath. As the great Indian scientist, Dr. A.P.J. Abdul Kalam, said: "Science and spirituality are two sides of the same coin. The Maha-Kumbh festival is a perfect example of this synergy." The following points highlight the scientific significance of Maha-Kumbh:

•Water Purification: Studies have shown that the ritual bathing in the sacred rivers during Maha-Kumbh has a positive impact on the water quality. The presence of certain microorganisms in the water has been found to have a self-purifying effect, reducing the levels of pollutants and bacteria. [7]

• Crowd Dynamics: Researchers have used Maha-Kumbh as a case study to understand crowd dynamics and behavior. By analyzing the movement patterns of large crowds, scientists have developed new models and algorithms to improve crowd management and safety during future festivals.

•Cultural Significance: Maha-Kumbh is a unique cultural phenomenon that provides a window into India's rich cultural heritage.

The festival is a celebration of India's diversity and pluralism, showcasing the country's rich cultural traditions and customs. Addressing the 118th episode of Mann Ki Baat and the first of this year, PM Modi said, "The Maha Kumbh has begun in Prayagraj. Unforgettable crowd, unimaginable scene and extraordinary confluence of equality and harmony... This time many divine yogas are also being formed in Kumbh. This festival of Kumbh celebrates unity in diversity. People from all over India and the world gather on the sands of Sangam. There is no discrimination or casteism anywhere in this tradition that has been going on for thousands of years. Everyone takes a dip in the Sangam, has a community feast together and takes Prasad together. That is why Kumbh is the Maha Kumbh of unity."

Studies have used ultra-modern research techniques, such as satellite imaging, GPS tracking, and big data analysis, AI powered surveillance systems , and Thousands of CCTV cameras and drones to study the movement of devotees and to ensure safery during the festival. These studies have provided valuable insights into the behavior and movement patterns of large crowds, which can be used to improve crowd management and safety during future festivals.[8]

Furthermore, scientific research has revealed the importance of the maha kumbh festival in terms of impact on the local ecosystem. Studies have shown that the festival helps to maintain the balance of the local ecosystem , with the ritual bathing helping to purify the water and reduce pollution.[9]

The use of ultra - modern research techniques has also revealed the significance of the mahakumbh festival in terms of its impact on the mental and physical health of devotees. Studies have shown that the festival has a positive impact on the mental health of devotees , reducing stress and anxiety and prompting a sense of well-being.

•Economic Importance of Maha-Kumbh"

The Maha-Kumbh festival has significant economic importance, both locally and nationally. The festival attracts millions of devotees and tourists, generating significant revenue for local businesses and the government. The festival also provides an opportunity for local artisans and craftsmen to showcase their wares and earn a livelihood. As the great Indian economist, Dr. Manmohan Singh, said: "The Maha-Kumbh festival is a shining example of the potential of tourism to drive economic growth and development." Studies have estimated that the Maha-Kumbh festival generates significant economic benefits, including:

- Increased tourism revenue
- Job creation and employment opportunities
- Increased demand for local goods and services.
- Improved infrastructure development.

The mahakumbh festival is expected to garner an estimated amount of rs. 2 lakh crore to 2.5 lakh crore (approximately $25 billion to $30 billion), which may account for about 0.8% of India's GDP[10][11]. Uttar Pradesh's GDP is expected to grow by over 1%. [12] Additionally , according to CIAT , approx rs. 45,000 crore is likely to be generated by local guesthouses, hotels , motels , restaurants, and more. However, the festival also poses significant economic challenges including :

- Managing the large crowds and providing adequate amenities.
- Ensuring the safety and security of devotees and tourists.
- Managing environmental impact of the festival.

Although all these challenges are managed by the help of scientific and ultra-modern research techniques. The mahakumbh festival contribute to economy in many ways, such as:

Foreign People Visiting Maha-Kumbh

•Cultural Exchange: Maha-Kumbh provides a unique opportunity for cultural exchange between India and the rest of the world. Foreign tourists can experience India's rich cultural heritage and spiritual traditions.

•Spiritual Seekers:

Many foreign tourists visit Maha-Kumbh in search of spiritual enlightenment and self-discovery. The festival provides a unique opportunity for spiritual seekers to explore India's rich spiritual traditions.

•	Tourism Revenue: Foreign tourists visiting Maha-Kumbh generate significant revenue for the local economy.
•	Increased Foreign Exchange Earnings:
•	Maha-Kumbh helps to increase India's foreign exchange earnings.[13]
•	Maha-Kumbh is providing Happiness and Well-being amidst the crisis all over the world:

•Stress Relief: Maha-Kumbh provides a unique opportunity for people to relieve stress and anxiety. The festival's spiritual atmosphere and rituals help to calm the mind and promote relaxation. [15][16]

•Sense of Community : Maha-Kumbh provides a sense of community and belonging for both national and foreign people. The festival brings people together, promoting social bonding and a sense of unity.[14]

•Spiritual Growth: The festival provides an opportunity for people to explore their spiritual side and promote spiritual growth. The festival's rituals and spiritual discourses help to promote self-awareness and self-discovery.

•Economic Benefits : Maha-Kumbh provides economic benefits to both national and foreign people. The festival generates revenue for local businesses and provides employment opportunities for thousands of people.

•Crisis Relief: Amid the crisis going on all over the world, Maha-Kumbh provides a sense of hope and relief. The festival's spiritual atmosphere and rituals help to promote a sense of calm and well-being, providing a much-needed respite from the crisis.

Conclusion

Mahakumbh has set new records in pilgrimage, infrastructure development, and exemplary sustainable development. Humongous population concentration at the Kumbha has not deterred the new pilgrims from paying the visit. Celebrities and pilgrims going and coming out with new excitement and fervor and their successful visits triggering more and more people to attend the event in itself shows an existence of a living strategy and a blueprint on sustainable coexistence. A sudden exponential surge and an equivalent surge to cater to this growth provides one with an exceptional opportunity of data analytics to be used in future. This data analytics readies a blueprint for the development of strategies for sustainable civilization. The most important dimensions in this strategy is offering adequate boarding/lodging, cleanliness, healthcare and hygiene which are important parameters for a sustainable civilization of the future.

In conclusion, the Maha-Kumbh festival holds immense spiritual, scientific, and economic importance, providing an opportunity for devotees to attain spiritual enlightenment and liberation, while also generating significant revenue for the local economy. As the great Indian sage, Swami Vivekananda, said: "The Kumbh Mela is a symbol of the eternal quest of the human soul for immortality and liberation."

Bibliography

Journals

Bhardwaj, S. M. (1973). Hindu places of pilgrimage in India; A study in cultural geography. University of California Press.

Chadha, H., & Onkar, P. (2016). Changing cities in the perspective of religious tourism – A case of Allahabad. Procedia Technology, 24, 1706–1713. https://doi.org/10.1016/j.protcy.2016.05.20 0

Chandan, S., & Kumar, A. (2019). Challenges for urban conservation of core area in pilgrim cities of India. Journal of Urban Management, 8(3), 472–484. https://doi.org/10.1016/j.jum.2019.05.001

David, S., & Roy, N. (2016). Public health perspectives from the biggest human mass gathering on earth: Kumbh Mela, India. *International Journal of Infectious Diseases, 47*, 42–45.

Forouhar, A., & Hasankhani, M. (2018). Urban renewal mega projects and residents' quality of life: Evidence from historical religious Center of Mashhad Metropolis. *Journal of Urban Health, 95*. https://doi.org/10.1007/s11524-017-0224-4

Greenough, P. G. (2013). The Kumbh Mela stampede: Disaster preparedness must bridge jurisdictions. *BMJ, 346*.

Holman, S. R., & Shayegan, L. (2014). Toilets and sanitation at the Kumbh Mela. http://www.who.int/healthinfo/global_burden_disease/metrics_daly/en/.

Houghton, R. A. (1994). The worldwide extent of land-use change. *BioScience, 44*(5), 305–313.

Kala, D., & Chaubey, D. S. (2023). Residents' perception and support before and after a mega-religious event during COVID-19 in India. *nternational Journal of Religious Tourism and Pilgrimage, 11*(1), 1–12. https://doi.org/10.21427/W5AK-H759

Kanaujiya, A. K., & Tiwari, V. (2022). Crowd management and strategies for security and surveillance during the large mass gathering events: The Prayagraj Kumbh Mela 2019 experience. *National Academy Science Letters, 45*(3), 263–273. https://doi.org/10.1007/s40009-022-01114-w

Web References:

1.   The Economics Times News, Jan 27, 2025
2.   Government of India , available at:
3.   https://www.mygov.in/campaigns/mahakumbh-2025/
4.   BS50 (business standard, available at https://www.business-standard.com/india-news/620-mn-devotees-visited-maha-kumbh-one-of-century-s-rarest-events-cm-yogi-125022300229_1.html
5.   Prayagraj district website, available at: https://prayagraj.nic.in/tourist-place/sangam/#:~:text=According%20to%20legends%2C%20Vishnu%20was,the%20devout%20can%20attain%20salvation.
6.   Prayagraj district website, available at: https://prayagraj.nic.in/tourist-place/sangam/#:~:text=According%20to%20legends%2C%20Vishnu%20was,the%20devout%20can%20attain%20salvation.
7.   By talking to people who visited there to take the holy dip in sangam.
8.   The Hindu , available at www.thehindu.com
9.   National library of Medicine, National Center for Biotechnology Information, available at: https://pubmed.ncbi.nlm.nih.gov/32146574/
10.   Ministry of Culture , available at https://pib.gov.in/PressReleaseIframePage.a

spx?PRID=2090956#:~:text=AI%20and%2
0Drone%20Surveillance%3A%20To,safety
%20during%20sacred%20Sangam%20Sna
n.

11.   Hindustan Times , available at
https://www.hindustantimes.com/ht-insight/
climate-change/how-maha-kumbh-can-insp
ire-environmental-change-1017387502183
43-amp.html

12.   Kotak securities, available at,
https://www.kotaksecurities.com/investing-
guide/articles/maha-kumbh-mela-2025-eco
nomic-impact/

13.   BW business world, available at ,
https://www.businessworld.in/article/bwtv-
breaking-down-the-mahakumbh-economy-
546029

14.   Ministry of Culture , available at,
https://pib.gov.in/PressReleaseIframePage.a
spx?PRID=2094640

15.   https://insideiim.com/current-affairs
-for-mba-exam/mahakumbh-mela-impact-o
n-tourism-and-economy

16.   Mahakumbh official website,
available at,
https://mahakumbh.in/oral-traditions-and-f
olklore-of-kumbh-mela/

17.   Deccan Herald , available at,
https://www.deccanherald.com/india/uttar-p
radesh/what-i-saw-at-the-maha-kumbh-mel
a-2-3407228

18.   Official website of Maha-Kumbh

19.	https://mahakumbh.in/product-tag/stress-relief/
20.	https://sundayguardianlive.com/maha-kumbh/a-profound-spiritual-odyssey

9 7 9 8 8 9 7 7 7 4 9 2 0